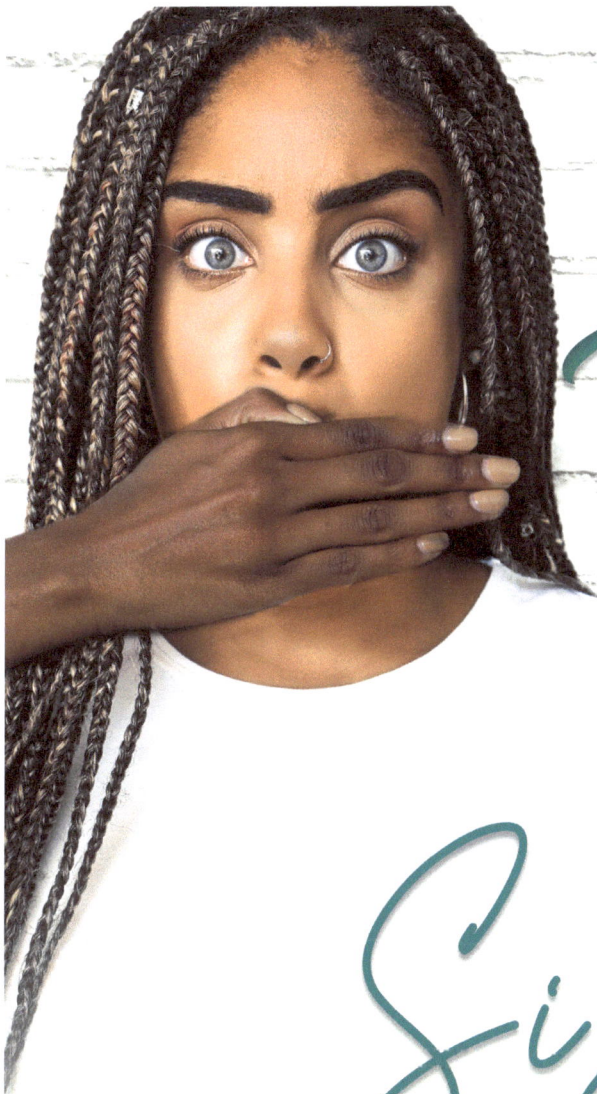

Ms. T. Lane

Sis,
WITH ALL DUE RESPECT
SHUT UP
AND LISTEN

SIS, WITH ALL DUE RESPECT

SHUT UP

AND LISTEN

MS. T. LANE

2

Other Work by the Author

Seductive Dreams: The Prophecy Begins

Seductive Dreams 2: The Prophecy Continues

Seductive Dreams 2: Alternate Ending

Sounds of Seduction: A Book of Poems

Dedication

I dedicate this book to:

My mother Teni D. Moore who taught me to never give up on my dreams and to fight for what is right. R.I.P mommy. I love you and I miss you very much.

To my grandparents Geri and LeeVada Moore, who raised me with stability, morals and integrity.

And to my children. Triniti and Dillon Jelks. I love you to the stars and beyond. Remember, shoot for the moon and you're guaranteed a star.

I Love All of You!

Acknowledgements

I'd like to thank all of my fans and supporters who didn't forget about me while I was away.

I want to thank God for answering my prayers, giving me the opportunity to grow and develop into the woman my soul always yearned to be.

I also want to thank everyone who purchased Sis, with All Due Respect, Shut-Up and Listen.

Thank You,

You are appreciated!

Much love and many blessings!

Preface

My gift of writing was developed as a coping mechanism to my mother's drug addiction. In 1998 I learned she relapsed after more than 10 years being clean. became angry and resentful, so I used that energy to create poetic words of grandiloquence (my favorite new word). Writing was the only thing that released the pain from climbing out of my body and jumping onto to someone else. I would write anywhere, on napkins at restaurants, on my hand, on bills anywhere. I can only describe it as an out of body experience, the words poured out of me like a cold glass Kool-Aid on hot summer day.

Watching my mother wither away was devastating, but I knew I could handle it and I knew it was not the worst thing I would have to deal with. I did everything I could to survive and out of that dark period came a light that could never be dulled.

I still use my writing as an outlet from heartache. When I say the ink from my pen symbolizes the blood draining from

my heart, I mean that shit. For real. I don't know how everyone else gets through their own personal trials and tribulations but if I hadn't discovered the talent of writing. I don't
think I would have survived. I pray that I continue with this gift
for the rest of my life and I hope to inspire others.

Be well and respect one another Queens!

~Ms. T. Lane

Contents

Introduction

 Okay, so I know this will be a hard pill to swallow and a challenging subject to tackle. When I decided to write "Sis, with All Due Respect, Shut Up and Listen," I knew it would be a heated topic, and it would ruffle a few feathers, but I also knew it needed to be said. Furthermore, it needed to be WRITTEN. In my experience, we don't listen very well. We tend to fly off the handle emotionally based on grandiloquence information presented as facts and or things we have come to accept as reality based on previous experiences. Now, don't get me wrong. We should use every occasion as a tool to get to the next level. Adventures in life are supposed to be used as a stepping-stone to get to higher ground and build a sturdy foundation. That does not mean that every ex-perience you have is precisely the same as the next, even if there are extreme similarities. Knowledge is powerful but knowing how and when to apply it is the real super-power. African American women (from now on, I will be referring to us as black) are born with super talents and powers that have guided our nation to many feats. Throughout history, black women stood by their men and stood behind them when that was necessary. Our strength and power don't need to be exerted or bragged about by shout-ing it to the holy heavens. If we take a look through-out history and pay attention to many of our black leaders, it can be agreed upon that at some point, conversations were being had with black women somewhere somehow. Whether it was a strong mother figure, sister, aunt, cousin, or wife, there was a powerful force remaining still like the weather on a dark, clear night. Although there is no rain or strong winds, you feel the essence and influence watching your every move.

When a black man needs advice and has nowhere to go, he seeks advice from a mother figure, wife, lover, or friend. We are the silent guide, the chess piece that slides across the board unnoticed, and by the time we are, it's likely too late for anything to be done about it. Our voices count to a high degree, but what I have been seeing is that we, as black women feel the need to stand on top of tables to get our voices heard. Yelling is not necessary when your voice is already a whisper in the background guiding the nation. If we are shouting to the high heavens trying to this means', there is so much focus on us getting our point across that we are not listening. We must learn to listen first; then, we can apply our knowledge and strength silently. Haven't the greatest battles been won when the enemy thought their opponent was sleeping or lying down on the job? I only use the war analogy because being a black woman is always a battle here in America. No matter who you are, where you come from, or how light your skin is. If you are a black woman here in America, you have felt the pain of racism one way or another. Sometimes it's so passive-aggressive you don't even notice it.

 I did not write this book to upset anyone or anger my black sisters. I am writing this book because, as a community, we have lost our way, and the only way we can get it back is to get our Nubian queen back on the throne. I have had several friends, and colleagues ask me how I did it. This question would always come about at different social events with my ex-husband, conversations amongst my male friends and their wives. For example, when I was getting married, one of my oldest friends asked me how I got my ex-husband to marry me. I was shocked at the question, and I responded with "nothing, he just wanted to marry me." I was only 24 years old when I got married, and it was my intention to get married before I had children. When my oldest friend asked me how I got my ex-husband to marry me, I don't think I quite understood the question. I am not sure if she thought there was a game or genuinely thought there was a secret recipe for making this happen. I realized that she honestly thought there was a se-cret that I carried, and I wasn't sharing it with her or anyone else for that matter. Today I can answer her question much better, and the secret was that I lis-tened. I listened to everything he told me. I was his confidant, his friend, and his guiding light.

I never ridiculed him for past mistakes, and I accepted him for the individual that he was. The one thing I know about black women is that we are very understanding when we listen. Listening is a superpower that gets over-looked and drained out when we want to make a point or when we demand our men to hear us. We must not allow our thoughts to overtake our minds so much that we do not listen and pay attention to what people (specifically our male counterparts) say. What you will find in this book, "Sis, with All Due Respect: Shut Up and Listen, are a few tools to help guide you when you are communicating with your boyfriend, husband, son, friend, or family member. The tools in this book are genuine gems that I have learned to use in my own life, and the difference I have noticed in responses when I am not listening vs. when I am, are opposites. So, *relax*, Sis, kick back and soak up this knowledge.

Chapter 1: Sis

I'd like to start the chapter by saying I wrote this book out of love for my sisters. I truly adore and admire every single one of you. Even the ones that are lost. Because in all of us, there is strength and power. When I come across a Sista that doesn't know her truth and power, my heart bleeds for her. I have to admit when my heart bleeds; there's no blood gushing from my chest. Instead, it shows up with acts of anger and words that could chop a man down faster than you can say timber. I learned at an early age that my words were my super-power. Early on, I was careless with my words and reckless when I used them. I understood how deep my words could cut a man, and when he hurt me, my words became my weapon of choice. I have learned a lot since then, and through-out my trials and tribulations, along with some helpful individuals that I listened to, I learned to be more careful with my words and my tone.

So, I have taken my idiosyncrasies into account and self -checked them at the beginning of this chapter. I am not perfect. I don't claim to be, and I have mad¹e my share of mistakes. The biggest one was not valuing who I was, being obnoxious, and arrogant about my talents/gifts. Due to my arrogance and disrespect to my craft, life found a way to humble me and bring me back to the person I was born to be. Being humbled by experience has its way of forcing you to listen to what the universe has to say. Now that I've had those experiences, it makes the self-check method much more comfortable when I come across a brilliant black woman who has dulled her life for one reason or another. If I come off a little

_____

judgmental, rigid, or over the top, please know it's coming from a place of love, and I genuinely want the best for us as a people. To do that, I know it starts with the givers of life, us, me, you, the goddess, the woman. Without Sista's, there are no kings. We are it! We are the ones (won's). Again, as you read these energetic words fit for several discussions, please remember the stories to solve a few of the issues we have with each other, our relationships, and to ratify our disdain.

Now that we've got that out of the way, let's get to the real nitty-gritty. The first issue I'd like to discuss is how we communicate with one another. The disrespect I have received from black women has left me feeling hostile, confused, and frustrated. So much so that I found myself conversing more with men than my sisters. As a black woman, I should have a conversation with one of my Sista's without feeling like anything I tell her can and will be used against me down the road. Now please don't get me wrong. Clearly, I understand there are good people and bad people, but when you value who you are as a person, these sabotage games are unnecessary. A black woman should never have to seek to destroy another black woman to gain success. Women that behave in this manner are one of the highest forms of loss. If tearing a woman down makes you feel like you have just won the U.S. Open, then I suggest that you try to heal whatever has hurt you and spend some time alone in deep meditation growing close to the Creator. Destroying another woman will only give you temporary pleasure, and then one day, you will find yourself suffering from the same nightmare that you once caused that woman. We must learn from each other. All of us were born with extraordinary gifts and powers. If we were to put all of our abilities together, we would dominate society, but we can't get past the next chicks fake Gucci Bag, and so what if it's fake, if you are not contributing to that woman's livelihood then, "Sis!" "With All Due Respect, Shut-Up and Listen." This is for you.

Before I get into dissing a woman about her apparel, I'd like to elaborate a little more about disrespect. I had pulled away from having any form of conversation with our black Sista's. It doesn't mean I chose another race in which to converse. I decided to remain silent and keep my words to myself because I found myself developing a disdain for my Sistas due to the level of disrespect I would receive. I mean, here I am looking at black women as goddesses, and we were behaving like devils amongst each other but then smiling and kissing the asses of the Becky's of the world. As a dedicated student of Black History, I understand the sickness, and I know it's deeper than just my generation. As a nation, we are broken. Let's start with slavery.

The trauma suffered during the dark times of slavery created severe psychological damage. Unfortunately, it's now a part of our D.N.A. When we start getting back on our feet in the '60s, and '70s, here comes another devastating blow-cocaine, heroin, PCP, and several other hallucinatory poisons somehow made its way to the suburban areas of Black Americans. During the time these drugs entered our communities, Black Americans were thriving. We were educators, secretaries, government officials, city employees, etc.; These people raised children to become successful, teaching them the trade tools and bringing them in as employees at their employers. Then all of a sudden, dope fled into our communities like a Tsunami. Every wave was hitting all of our affluent neighborhoods (reminiscent of black wall street), taking with it the sons and daughters of prominent political officials and hard-working black Americans. The destruction of our communities was by no means an accident or some strange coincidence. Th^{2}e government and people in charge of this country planned the downfall of our people. It was a systematic approach to destroy the prominent Black American Family.

Next came the guns and gang banging. As if it wasn't hard enough watching our beautiful black sisters', mothers, daughters, brothers, uncles, fathers do some of the most horrific things to get the next hit. We had to watch them kill each other to get the dope fiends dollar. Humph. Crazy. When you sit back and think about how dangerous we must be, we became the Gods and Goddesses we know we can be. Now that we are slowly working our way out of the gangs and cocaine, the police have started WWIII on our young black brothers and sisters. It's like to matter what; there is no escape for the young black Amer-I-CAN trying to live a successful life.

I didn't mean to go into a tangent about race because that is not what this book is referencing. Still, to get my Sista's back on board with each other, we have[3] to understand first and foremost that we are under attack, and the system will wage war against us in every and any way possible. Including the Criminal Justice system, which has been locking up our young black men for years, and somehow the women raised the children with dignity and respect although their fathers were serving a life sentence. Now that we've proven we can still make something out of ourselves without our fathers being 100 percent present in the home. They have now sunken

---

their claws into the Family Law Justice system. First, they went after our black men with a thing called child support. It is locking them up for the so-called not taking care of their children(s) law. Now, this is a complete and utter fabrication. Of course, you will find dead beats in every culture, but this is not the black community's overall majority, contrary to belief. Yes, some black men do not take care of their children, but this has been the case for centuries, stemming from slavery. There would be a man that made babies with a woman, then gets free and forgets all about his children. I am no saying it is okay for men to make babies and leave them; it is not okay. I want to make it very clear that most black men do not make babies and leave them. I am not sure where that concept is derived, but it's a fallacy. The statistics will say something different, but ask yourself, who's creating the statistics?

Black men take care of their kids, and except for the crack epidemic that flooded our communities, they have always naturally taken care of their children. If you took a look back throughout history and skipped the crack epidemic, you will find that 90% of the black households had mothers and fathers. We became broken when crack came along. When I say, take a look back. Please don't do a google search; I mean taking a look back. Look back at your family history, take a look at your grandfathers, great grandfathers. The majority of us had them. So, if black men don't take care of their children, how can most black people tell you their grandfather's name and tell you what his favorite acholic drink was. We have to stop allowing them to tell our stories. WE lived it, and WE know the truth, but I digress. Let's get back to the family law system. So, we know that crack, gangs, and guns destroyed our community,

30

and in the '80-'90s a lot of our black men (thanks to Joe Biden and the Clinton administration) were in prison, and this left the mothers to raise the children. As women, we were doing pretty good with raising our black boys and girls. We were once again getting back on top. The legal way. Whether we were gaining the upper hand in sports, music, or even just the average 9-5, we were coming back as a community. In the 2000's they have created a brand-new way to destroy the black family, and that's with the Family Law (In) Justice system, and I can tell you first-hand. There is no justice at all in this courtroom, and in a lot of ways, it's worse than the criminal justice system because it's a silent killer. No one pays attention to it, and quite frankly, no one gives a damn! The malarky that happens in this courtroom is beyond what anyone could believe. I have sat in on cases and watched a judge systematically destroy families one by one. They use the father's fear of paying child support to allow him to move his chess pieces around the board illegally and unethically. The rule-makers don't follow their own rules, and quite frankly, they don't even apply. Children are snatched from their mother's bosom as if a child never needed it's mothers breast milk to survive. The bond between a mother a child is broken forever, like the missing link in your favorite chain. I experienced this when my daughter was only nine years old, and my son was a budding three-year-old boy. I was 33 years old, handling a tumultuous divorce on my own, dealing with my mother's untimely death, working full time for a well-established car company, and going to school, plus raising my kids 70% of the time on my own. I have never touched any drug in my life, and my children have always been my top priority. Never once have I ever put my children in harm's way. Somehow, I found myself with 8 hours of visitation with my children for no reason other than some fictitious story my ex-husband provided to the crooked commissioner so he could get full custody with hopes of never having to pay child support. Which is one thing I never wanted from him ever. I came from the old school, which meant that I followed a code. That meant that even if I struggled, I wouldn't be asking him for child support. I had a loving family, and if my ex wanted to dip off into the wind, he would be the one missing out on two wonderful and highly intelligent beings. Filing for child support in the courts or even through the system was never an option and something I never did. I even forfeited my alimony. I won't go too much into detail about my personal story, but I am not alone in this Family Law struggle. The system has once again found a way to use US against US. On the outside, it looks like we are killing each other in the streets in gang wars, but you and I know what's going on (courtesy of Tupac Amaru Shaku R.I.P). It seems like black men are taking children away from black women, but we also know how that started. Child support has done nothing but destroys our community, and it was never necessary to make a black man pay for raising his children. Just pay attention to history. Even in our movies, the harsh Menace II Society, Boyz in the hood, Tray's main character had an active father in his life. When he became of age and was getting out of hand, his mother willingly handed him over to his father. We, as women, never needed child support. We know how to get what we want without having the system solve our problems for us. Black Women are powerful, and we don't need the government's help to get our black men in order. We can handle them. We have to realize that we are the power. Black men have and will always listen to us. Even when we believe they aren't. As of today, my ex-husband and I have zero forms of communication (not my choice), and somehow, I can get everything I want and need for our children. I don't even have to see or speak to him again, but I know how to get him to listen. I am the power and the light. He will always follow my lead.

Sis, wake up and realize who you are. Don't let your power get muted. You are the Krazy glue that holds this entire nation together. You matter way more than you think, and, on that note, I am going to move on to the next order of business.

Keyboard Gangsters. If you are a keyboard gangster, please stop. Nobody believes you. If you are the person who spouts disrespectful rhetoric on Facebook (to other black women) and other social media platforms, you are a coward to the fullest extent of the word. Now I know that some of the people behind the keyboards are either bots or just misinformed individuals who have no clue about the topics they are discussing. Recently, I had an experience worthy of writing. There was a Facebook post about black boys learning to behave like women. I usually don't get involved in these types of bait posts, but I was intrigued and decided to dance with the devil, so I asked the person who posted the message which was raising these boys to be women? Is it the men or the women? This post went unanswered for several days, and finally, someone decided to respond. The response came from a woman with the profile pic displaying a young sister, maybe early 20's. Her response to me was that I was irrelevant, and I had no level of understanding. My profile pic clearly shows me sitting at the table with books, so this felt more like a set up than anything else (even without this pic, she never should have typed the words she typed to a fellow sister); however, I indulged. I laid down the law and explained that she needed to know who she was dealing with before she stepped to someone of my stature. At this point, I became the prime enemy. Next came insults about my work, who I was as a person, and several reasons I deserved to be spoken to so rudely. I became frustrated because we didn't talk to each other when I was growing up, and we didn't disrespect older black women. Whether they were educated or not, just the mere fact that they lived through the things they lived through gave them a badge of honor, and we never stepped over that line. We didn't correct our elder women, and we damn sure didn't disrespect them in any shape or fashion. Today these young girls say and do whatever they want. They never think about the struggle the person they are speaking with may have overcome. The things I have seen, experienced, and triumphed are enough to silence an entire army, but here this young girl was talking to me as if she had leveled up overnight and became a general commanding a nation. After about 3 or 4 intellectual exchanges (all on my part), she silently bowed out. I am sure Maya Angelou, Oprah Winfrey, Rosa Parks, Afeni Shakur, Assata Shakur, etc., never had to write a book about how disrespectful her counterparts were or even had to check the ones coming up under them. I am not a huge fan of Oprah, but I know the work she put in helped several generations of women, including myself. If there were no Maya Angelou, there would be no Ms. T. Lane. Our pieces are very different, but I respect her to the fullest extent of the word; I would never address Maya Angelou (R.I.P.) as Maya. I appreciated her to the highest degree, and somehow, we have learned that disrespecting each other is okay, then we jump on the bandwagon of the person doing the disrespect. What is this behavior, and from where did it come? We ridicule each other because one person may be lower than the next, we laugh at each other because one person's hair is nappier than the next person's, we bash each other when an-other Sista doesn't meet our standard of perfection. This kind of behavior needs to stop, and if you are doing this, "Sis, With all Due Respect." "Shut-Up and Listen!" This book is for you.

The next level of pure disrespect is the in-person disrespect that I have seen women do to other women. I can't say that Sista's have disrespected me directly, but I am quite sure it has happened to me indirectly; however, the moment I don't acknowledge it, they move on to their next victim. I have seen per-sonal disrespect happen several times over. One time I was at a social event sitting with a group of women, and then another woman walked into the room. Immediately this group of women began to tear the other woman down piece by piece. From her hair weave to the bottom of her shoes. I understand this type of psychosis has been happening for years, and I also understand this is something that women do, but it's more than just a free spirit laughs at someone else's expense, its pure self-hate. We hate each other because we see a piece of ourselves in that person. There is a level of admiration behind every hateful word, and instead of showing love to each other, we spout out rude remarks and tear each other down. If the Sista has on cheap shoes that you know is embarrassing her, maybe she honestly doesn't know anything else and if she doesn't know, try taking her shopping with you. Build her up to don't tear her down. Our people have broken in so many ways, and the only way we can begin proper reparations is to start with our women. We must confide in each other, trust each other when we have bad days, and hold each other accountable when we are out of line, which is practiced very well in the Muslim community. Don't get me wrong; Muslims have their fair share of emotional rollercoasters when it comes to women, but RESPECT'ing each other is held to the highest level, and they correct each other. We are so afraid to tell each other the truth these days that we will allow our sisters to go out in the world and ruin their lives because we don't want to hear her response. We do not think that this woman may bear children somewhere down the line and interact with our descendants. There are only six degrees of separation, and at some point, your offsprings will run across that sister's offspring, and if you did your job correctly, you would be the guiding light that brought people together. If you didn't do your job, then the six degrees may not fathom too well for your offspring.

We have to be healthy and brave enough to deal with the backlash that comes with correction, and on the flip side, we also have to know when to Shut up and Listen. It doesn't sound effortless on paper, but we followed the code when we were a nation of our own, and the men respected us. In other cultures, they follow the code. Women love each other even when they don't like each other. They remain strong together because they know what can happen when the woman loses her sense of power. We are the ones with all the power, and yet we are walking around doing everything we can to use it on each other. Wow! Isn't that something? If we are powerful enough to destroy each other, imagine how power-ful our nation would be if we started loving each other. Now how do we get there is the question—my suggestion. Learn to love yourself first. No one on this planet, not your son, your daughter, your boy-friend, no one can love you as you can. Instead of doing things to impress others, how about you do something to impress who you are.

Free yourself from whatever society has boggled you down. A weave isn't that important, and for whom are you doing it? REAL men don't care about what your hair looks like or what your nails look like daily. Now, if he's presenting you at some different event, but in the grand scheme of things, you are dressing up to outdo the next woman. That seems a little bi-sexual to me but then go ahead if you like that kind of thing. If you are genuinely a straight woman, stop doing things to impress the next fe-male. If you want to get your nails done because it pleases you, then do it for that reason and that rea-son alone.

You are trying to outdo the next woman that you will soon be cackling about with your girlfriends. I can't stand talking about other women unless it per-tains to their effect on me. Listen, if a woman isn't having a direct impact on my livelihood, then I have nothing at all to say about her. Sis, if you find your-self obsessing about another woman and speaking negatively about her for no apparent reason, "With All Due Respect, Shut Up! And Listen. It's time to grow up, be the woman you always dreamt you could be, and if you didn't dream of being a better woman, I am telling you today that you can. It starts with you.

Chapter 2: With All Due Respect

Sometimes we have to "Destroy to Rebuild" (courtesy of YG Hootie, one of Compton's finest.) If it requires me to destroy the black woman's current image to get my Sista's back, then consider it destroyed. The image we have of the black woman is this bad BITCH with a body like Megan Thee Stallion, and she is today's role model. The women in Africa don't even look like her. We have to understand the history of the African. First and foremost, Africa is a huge continent, and all the people do not look the same. They all come from different areas, and they all have tribes. Every tribe has its signature look. Africans used to be able to verify a person's identity specifically by looking at them. The women that were stacked were from certain tribes, and their bodies served a purpose. For example, the Creator designed those women's bodies based on the lands and or the man's needs. Some men in Africa have a Huge Penis. An average woman cannot handle that man. Every living thing on this planet serves a purpose, and the Creator designed every natural body shape for a real reason. Now we have today women like Megan Thee Stallion recreating God's work. It shouldn't be this way. Every man cant be for every woman and vice versa. Just because you want to look like the women from the Zulu tribe doesn't mean you can. You become a fake and an imposter (something I too had to understand) if you do.

There are also women like Lizzo, Nikki Minaj, and dare I say the O.G. that started it all, Little Kim. Little Kim is the hardest one to name in this list because I grew up around people who adored her and her music. I was not a fan and never wanted to be like her, but somehow out of all the nasty things she said, I grew to understand her and later came to respect her. She's a real one, but she is responsible for the Nikki Minaj's of the world; however, she is also a human being. It's challenging for me to categorize her with these other black women who degrade themselves for money. Little Kim's story seems like it was more than attention-seeking. She seemed to me like she was under the influence of a man she respected to a very high degree and would do anything for him. Which is not the same as the individuals mentioned above. Since Megan Thee Stallion seems to be it girl, I will focus on her and how she behaves. If we as black women accept her as our children's role model, we will become her or something much worse. I already know what you will combat this argument with, and it's that same old hood statement. "That bitch making money." And you would be right, yes, she is, but you have to give up something to get the money. Normally it's an exchange of time. Like a job. You give up your time, and your boss pays you for it. What is Megan Thee Stallion giving up? No one on this planet can convince me that she is okay with men gawking at her every chance they get. Men are extremely disrespectful when they see a woman displaying themselves the way she does. They see sex, and that is all they see. The moment she pretends that's not what she is, they make her pay for it, one way or another. Although she is collecting that fat paycheck, we all know as women that it doesn't feel good to be sexualized all the time. Now and then, we like to feel sexy, but unwanted attention from strange men gawking at our beautiful bodies is not a good feeling. It feels like a form of rape every time; there is an unwanted sexual advance thrown your way. All because you dressed in clothing displaying your nice round behind and your nice round bosoms. Black women are beautiful. We come in many shapes, colors, and sizes. Now at almost 40 years old, I can understand why black men have trouble being faithful. I mean, how could you even expect that with all of the beautiful goddesses walking around here freely. My idea of beauty is not Megan Thee Stallion. My idea of beauty is Claire Huxtable. My role model. Now she was the epitome of poise, style, elegance, and beauty. Even though she was a fictional character, she was this woman in real life. She had standards, morals, and class. Even if she did something unbecoming. No one knew about it. Claire Huxtable was the woman I wanted to be, the woman I am becoming, and the woman I have always admired. Somehow our nation has switched from wanting to be like Claire to wanting to be Megan Thee Stallion. When I was growing up, none of

50

the women would have ever allowed us to behave like a Megan Thee Stallion. I grew up in a community where, if a girl was doing nasty things with a boy, the community had a conversation with the parent. Today people are so afraid to get involved that they let the children of our future throw their lives away right in front of them without saying a word. Today the older women in our community will see a young 12-year old girl going down on a grown man and turn their heads around to gossip about her to the next woman that will listen. These are the same children that will have an impact on our livelihoods in the future. Whether they become a politician or if it's just their vote. Their decisions can have a direct impact on our lives. So why are we a nation of brilliant black women allowing these things to occur? My answer, we don't love ourselves enough to love anyone else. Society has broken the black American Family, and

to make the pain go away, we (as women) seek outside attention, which leads to further self -destruc-
tion. We will never get love outside of ourselves. We
find true love in our hearts, and once we do that, we
are limitless to the things we can do. We can't work
with each other, we can't go into business together,
and we can't share our plans due to the jealousy and
hatred amongst us. Sis, if this is you, "With All Due
Respect, Shut-Up!" "And Listen." This is for you.

To destroy and rebuild is simple. It's not rocket
science, and we don't have to reinvent the wheel. All
we have to do is start loving ourselves uncondition-
ally, and the rest will fall into place. We don't trust
each other because we have burned each other, but
we will authorize a man over and over again, no matter how many times he burns us. Now don't get me
wrong, some women you will never trust, but we

have to try and get along with each other for our future generations to have a better life than we currently have today. Let's start by going into business together. Write up a contract to be sure no one is getting had or played. Hire a trust-worthy black attorney to draw up the paperwork if you have a family member that's an even better attorney. I am not a huge fan of attorneys mainly because I know more than I should about their work line, but if you pay them to draw up the contract, just double-check the details or, if necessary, create your own. All kinds of websites allow you to create a legally binding agreement. Black women do not do well in corporate America. The corporations know we are the genius' behind their products. They know we suffer from the damage America caused our community, and we are pleased when they reward us for our contributions to their companies, so they give us the most problems.

They never want to see you grow beyond your current position, so they will provide you with verbal praise, reward you with paper certificates, make you an employee of the month. Still, when it's time for an increase in salary or a promotion, they say you have a bad attitude. Even if you are that rarity and you do get a promotion. At what cost were you promoted? Did they encourage you just to keep your Sista's in line? Did they encourage you because they needed a Sista on the board to make them look like an EOE? Everyone is afraid of Tameka with the Dookey braids becoming C.E.O of the company. I have yet to see "Tamika" on anyone's cover page for C.E.O. of the year.

I am saying all of this because America has enticed the black woman to come to their workforce by paying us dollar figures that our hard-working blue-collar counterparts cannot make on their own. America is paying the black woman with a Highschool education anywhere from $25hr-$35hr entry-level. Now I am all for the Sista's getting that bag, and if you are single, I say bring it, but if you are in a relationship and you become the breadwinner, this can become a huge problem even when it seems like it's not. The system will steal, kill, and destroy our families by any means necessary (Malcolm X). We have to know this, be aware of this, and act upon this. The best thing for us to do right now is to start our businesses. Run our beauty supply stores, operate our hair and nail salons. The money is available to us. We just have to get it.

We also have to stop our children from becoming the real Megan Thee Stallion and Lizzo's. Although they may be successful in their careers, this is not the way to go. We have to get our respect back from our men and then from America. Right now, the black woman is THEE most disrespected woman on the planet, and nobody gives a damn! Let's do something about it, and Sis, if you are a Lizzo or Megan Thee Stallion, *Shut-Up, and Listen*, this is for you!

Chapter 3: Shut Up And Listen!

Now before you get all bent out of shape and start rolling your eyes, don't be mad at the Shut-Up chapter. I dedicate this chapter to all those women who just don't know when to quit. I will admit I have said some pretty harsh things to my male counterparts that I should never have said. I've said something to men in a jokingly manner that probably hurt them more than any angry word ever could. I am not a naturally mean person, but if a man does something unmanly, I have a way of making him feel like he is less than a human being. Not a good thing, and I am not bragging or boasting about it at all. I am only revealing this information because there are times when I, too, need to SHUT-UP! I dedicate this chapter to my mother, Teni D. Moore (R.I.P.); she used to tell me all the time that I just didn't know when to Shut Up! And

I would still argue my position after she told me to shut-up!

The thing is that I would only argue my point if I knew I was right, meaning I followed up with evidence or some sort of reassurance. It didn't help my mother in dealing with me. All it did was anger her more. If she would say her famous line, "You just don't know when to shut-up, do you!" I would respond with, "Why should I? I'm right." My poor mother, she had a lot to handle dealing with me at 16 years old. The point is whether you are right or wrong, you must have a stop button, especially in our relationships. Hitting a man over the head with the same thing over and over again only makes him want to get as far away from you as possible, even if you *are* right. I have noticed the best way to win an argument with a man is to state your position and move on from it. Say what you have to say about the situation and move on to the next point. Believe me; he heard you the first three times you said it. If you continue to criticize him, he has a few options. Depending on his temper, he may knock the shit out of you, simply walk away and never return, or my favorite that my ex consistently used on me.

Just agree with you and then have an affair with some strange woman either that night or the next. We have to know when to Shut Up. Our words really can hurt these men, and although they act like they are stronger than the earth's core, they are more sensitive than we are. Again, we are representations of their mothers. If they love us and we bash them into the ground, we will destroy a piece of them each time we do it. They hurt; they feel just like we do. Even if the situation isn't as serious as an argument, let's say, for example, your significant other comes home discussing an incident at work, and you are not happy with the way he handled it. Don't tell him he was wrong and don't offer your opinion unless he asks for your opinion.

Just be an ear for him to lend a story. Stop and listen, and I mean, listen carefully. Most of the time, we already know what went wrong by understanding the outcome, but they don't always need to hear what they did wrong or how they should have handled it. Sometimes they just want their woman to listen and hear them out. Stop offering your opinion and judging him. If you feel the need to tell him everything he should have done, he is not the one for you. Not all men are Alpha males, and some of them want you to tell them what to do but wait until he asks. He will be much more receptive to your response if he asks for the information versus volunteering it.

The best thing you could ever do in a relationship with a man is listening to him. Most men don't talk a whole lot so listen to him when he speaks. Give him the attention he's asking. Allow him to lead if he's a leader. I know some men are not born leaders, and nowadays, many women are showing the relation-ships. If that's your personal preference, then Sis, you go right ahead, but for the rest of us that love an Alpha male, we have to let them be the Alpha male. A relationship can't work with an Alpha male and a so-called Alpha female.

Ladies, I ask again that you be careful with your words when dealing with your significant other. You can destroy or build a man. If you use it to knock them down, it will return to you like a ton of bricks. People have told me that I am mean, and I say what-ever I want out of my mouth. For years I never thought there was anything wrong with it because why? You guessed it. I was right. I shouldn't have been so careless with my words, and if I had known what I know now, I would never have said the things that I said. Sometimes it wasn't what I said but the way I said it along with my tone. My voice is powerful, and it can give life or destroy life. I made the change and decided I wanted to breathe life into things instead of taking it away. I can't say that I was deliberately mean, calculated or bitter. These are not qualities I possess, but I can say that I was irresponsible with my power. It took me to develop my talents, be humbled by this thing called life. That's when I realized who I was and the strength I had. Once I began to believe in myself, I focused my energy on empowering our kings and breathing life back into them. Even those who don't think they are Kings because no one should ever wake up feeling undervalued.

When your man is trying to watch the 49ers, the game lets him do it without bothering him, especially if his friends are over. Suppose you are the kind of woman that likes to wear skimpy clothing when your husbands' friends come over, Sis with All Due Respect, STOP and listen. Not only are you disrespecting him, but you are doing yourself an injustice. The best thing you could ever do for your man is to make him feel like the King in his domain. If you step into a room full of his friends with skimpy clothing, it looks like you are available for not just your husband but his friends too, and if you think that one of them won't try it, think again. When I was a little girl, my grandfather would have poker parties in the den with all of his buddies. I could not go back there, and his wife was only allowed to bring them whatever it was they needed to drink on. I know this sounds a little archaic, but it worked for our family, and I didn't turn out so bad. When my grandmother delivered whatever alcoholic beverage she was serving my grandfather and his friends, she was not wearing her bedclothes. Some things you just have to know not to do in front of other men. It seems like common sense, but common sense ain't that common.

Oh, and sis, don't have sex with your hus-band/boyfriends' friends. It may seem like the thing to do now, or it may seem like the best get back re-venge type of thing, but this will ALWAYS come back to bite you in the butt. Back in my day, this may have been a little easier to get away with because the woman could always say it was a lie, but with social media and all of these secret recording devices ain't nobody getting away with anything anymore. If you choose to go down this slippery slope, you will lose all respect from all parties involved (including your self-respect), and you will become the biggest whore on the planet. Whether you are or not doesn't matter at all. You could have been a virgin before sleeping with either of them, but the minute you bed, your man's friend, you are asking for a heap of trouble. Even if he says, he is okay with it. Don't believe it. It's a setup. I don't care if you guys dated in high school, then you fall for his friend that you all knew together in high school, don't do it. You will be flushing your power right down the toilet, and he nor his friend will look at you the same. They will secretly share jokes about you behind your back, or worse, they may not say anything to each other at all, but somehow someway they will make you pay for it.

So, I think this pretty much sums it for Sis, With All Due Respect, Shut-Up, and Listen. I know some of the things were very strong and hard to discuss, but that's the problem. We have stopped having hard conversations, and we need to get back to that. Now to all of my Sista's turning their noses up at this book, let me give you a little bit of background on myself and explain why I am a self-proclaimed expert on this topic. I was married for 14 years, and during that marriage, it produced two beautiful children, a girl, and a boy. I had the perfect family until my ex-husband's adulterous affairs took a toll on me. After his 3rd unprotected affair, I decided my life was worth more than what I was getting out of it, and in 2013 I filed for divorce. I had great times in my marriage and my wedding day was beautiful.

I was happy most of my marriage, but when I be-came unhappy most of my latter days, I knew it was time to call it quits. I had more good times than bad, and I am not mad at my experience. It happened, and now it's not happening. I am okay with it. I am sharing that information because I believe in mar-riage, and I can say the only thing I did wrong was not communicating correctly with my ex-husband, and if you ask him, I am sure he will tell you the same. If I had worked on my communication skills, maybe he wouldn't have had the affairs, to begin with, or perhaps he would have. Whichever one I still should have communicated better, it would have changed many things, including how he handled me in the divorce. Now enough about that. I genuinely hope this short piece helps many women deal with the men in their lives. Once we get our behavior in check, we are going to take over the world.

-Peace-

~Ms. T. Lane

Note from Ms. T. Lane

I would like to take a moment to thank you and let you know I truly appreciate you taking the time out of your busy schedule to read my book. Without readers, there are no writers. It poses the question, *"If a book is written and no one reads it was ever really written at all?" (Ms. T. Lane)*

I appreciate every single one of you supporting my work. Thank You, and I wish you peace and happiness.

Blessings Kings and Queens. Until next time.........

~Ms. T. Lane

Words of encouragement.

I was born out of wedlock to two teenage parents. My mother had just turned 16 before giving birth to me, and my father was about to be 18 years old a few weeks after my arrival. Both my mother and father would both become addicted to drugs. My grandparents raised me (beautiful people), but they were not my parents. I grew up feeling empty, thrown away like a piece of garbage, and later, I would find out that my mother was ready to sell me for a piece of crack until my father stepped in.

I grew up in Compton, California. An area that is well known for gang activity, and I later relocated to another Ghetto called the "Jungles."

I was supposed to be a statistic. I am the one America couldn't stop. I dodged teenage pregnancy, baby daddy drama, received my Highschool Di-

ploma, completed college, got married, and produced two beautiful children from that marriage.
Now, I can add a successful author to my resume. I
am saying all of this to say that just because you
come from nothing doesn't mean you are nothing.
Sometimes nothing from nothing can equal something. "*I am that something.*" Even a zero has a de-
fining purpose. *"You can't get to a million without
the zero."*

Queen, believe in yourself, trust yourself. You
were born with all the answers!

I send you this message with all the love in the
universe. If I can do it, so can you!

Ms. T. Lane

Follow Ms. T. Lane

Website: WWW.MSTEELANE.COM

Facebook: www.Facebook.com/MsTeeLane

Instagram: www.instagram.com/missteelane

Other Works by the Author:

1. Seductive Dreams: The Prophecy Begins

2. Seductive Dreams 2: The Prophecy Continues

3. Seductive Dreams: Alternative Ending

4. Sounds of Seduction: A Book of Poems